TRUE or FALSE?

This worm can grow up
to four feet (1.2 m)
long—in your body!

3/08

CL

TRUE!

Female guinea worms can grow up to four feet (1.2m) long.

Guinea worm disease occurs mostly in Africa. People can get it when they drink water that contains a very small flea that hosts an even smaller guinea worm.

The guinea worm then grows inside the human body. After about a year, the worm comes out—through the skin.

To find out about other dangerous worms— and the people who fight them—keep reading.

Book design Red Herring Design/NYC

Library of Congress Cataloging-in-Publication Data
Tilden, Thomasine E. Lewis, 1958–
Belly-busting worm invasions! : parasites that love your insides! /
by Thomasine E. Lewis Tilden.
p. cm. — (24/7: science behind the scenes)
Includes bibliographical references.
ISBN-13: 978-0-531-12068-2 (lib. bdg.)   978-0-531-18736-4 (pbk.)
ISBN-10: 0-531-12068-6 (lib. bdg.)   0-531-18736-5 (pbk.)
1. Intestines—Parasites—Juvenile literature. I. Title.
RC119.7T55 2007
616.3'407—dc22   2006005876

© 2008 Scholastic Inc.
All rights reserved. Published by Franklin Watts, an imprint of Scholastic Inc.

Published simultaneously in Canada. Printed in the United States of America.

BELLY-BUSTING WORM INVASIONS!

Parasites That Love Your Insides!

Thomasine E. Lewis Tilden

WARNING: If pages 1 and 2 grossed you out, you're in trouble. This book is crawling with worms and flesh-eating parasites. Slither through it at your own risk.

Franklin Watts
An Imprint of Scholastic Inc.
New York • Toronto • London • Auckland • Sydney
Mexico City • New Delhi • Hong Kong
Danbury, Connecticut

CONTENTS

These cases are 100% real. Find out how infectious disease doctors solved these medical mysteries.

A little worm is big trouble in the country of Ghana.

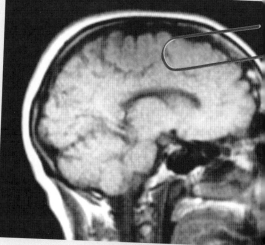

Something has invaded a woman's brain in CA.

Can a sand fly from Peru eat a man's face?

MEDICAL DOWNLOAD

Here's even more amazing stuff about parasites for you to ingest.

YELLOW PAGES

Think of parasites as the worst guests ever. They arrive for a visit—and may never leave.

MEDICAL 411

They never bring their hosts anything helpful. But they will snatch whatever they can from their hosts' bodies—including blood cells, tissue, and bone. If parasites aren't stopped, they can seriously injure—or even kill—their hosts.

IN THIS SECTION:

▶ how infectious disease specialists really talk;

▶ how parasites invade bodies;

▶ and the kinds of people working to prevent and treat diseases caused by parasites.

Parasite Hunters

Infectious disease specialists have their own way of speaking. Find out what their vocabulary means.

infectious disease doctor
(in-FEK-shuhss duh-ZEEZ DOK-tur) a medical doctor who is an expert in diseases caused by parasites, bacteria, viruses, and fungi

Let's call in an infectious disease doctor to look at this patient.

blood test
(blud test) a close examination of a patient's blood to determine if there are any parasites or unusual features in the blood

In the meantime, let's do a blood test on the patient.

microscopic
(mye-kruh-SKOP-ik) describing something so small it can only be seen under a microscope

Uh-oh. The lab thinks they've found a microscopic— but dangerous— parasite in the patient's blood.

parasite
(PA-ruh-site) an animal or plant that gets its food by living on or inside a plant, animal, or other organism

If I had to guess, I'd say the parasite has given the patient a bad infection.

infection
(in-FEK-shun) when a body part is invaded with a disease caused by parasites, viruses, fungi, or bacteria

Our **host organism**—this patient here—is being eaten alive!

host organism
(hohst OR-guh-niz-uhm) any life-form—like a plant or animal—where a parasite lives

Say What?

Here's some other lingo an infectious disease specialist might use on the job.

contaminated
(kuhn-TAM-uh-nay-tid) made dirty or unfit for use
*"The water has been **contaminated** with parasites."*

diagnose
(dye-uhg-NOHSS) to figure out what disease a patient has
*"We've never seen a case of leishmaniasis here. That's why it was so hard to **diagnose**."*

eradicate
(ih-RAD-uh-kate) to get rid of completely
*"We're determined to **eradicate** that disease from the face of the earth."*

transmitted
(trans-MIT-tid) passed on; spread
*"Malaria is **transmitted** by mosquito bites."*

Unwelcome Guests

Here's a look at some parasites you'd definitely rather not meet in person.

	PARASITE	HOST	HOW YOU CAN GET IT	WHERE YOU CAN GET IT
	giardia intestinalis	humans	by swimming in a lake or stream and drinking the water	anywhere there are lakes or streams
	taenia solium (pork tapeworm)	inside pigs	by eating pork infected with the parasite	anywhere people eat pork
	leishmaniasis	in sand flies	by getting bitten by a sand fly	deserts and jungles—mostly in India, Bangladesh, Nepal, Sudan, and Brazil
	guinea worm (also called dracunculiasis)	in water fleas	by drinking water infected with the fleas	countries in Asia and Africa

WHERE IT LIVES IN HUMANS	WHAT THE SYMPTOMS ARE	HOW IT'S DIAGNOSED	TREATMENT
intestines and stomach	diarrhea, stomachache, bloating, weight loss	by examining stool samples	medication
brain, eye tissue, liver	In the brain, it causes **seizures** and **lesions**. In other areas it can cause sores.	by scanning (taking pictures of) the area	medication. Sometimes surgery is needed for eye or brain infections.
begins in the intestines and travels to the mouth and nose areas	raised sores on skin, filled with yellow **pus**. Patients usually have fever and weight loss.	by testing the pus and blood; checking for enlarged spleen and liver	medication
first in the stomach. Then it travels— usually to the legs and feet.	itchy, burning sensation when worm starts to come out of human's skin	by seeing blisters where worms have created openings; also, by seeing the worms emerge	slowly twisting the worm around a stick until it is completely out of the body

The Medical Team

Infectious disease doctors are part of a team. Here's a look at some of the health-care workers who help solve medical mysteries.

INFECTIOUS DISEASE DOCTORS
They specialize in diseases caused by parasites, bacteria, viruses, and fungi.

NEUROLOGISTS
They are doctors who specialize in diseases of the brain and nervous system.

INTERNAL MEDICINE DOCTORS
They are usually the first doctors patients see. They can identify problems and call in other specialists.

RADIOLOGISTS
They take and interpret x-rays and other tests that show the inside of patients' bodies.

VOLUNTEERS
They help educate people about how to prevent and treat infectious diseases.

CLINICAL PATHOLOGISTS
They examine patients' blood and tissue under a microscope.

TRUE-LIFE CASE FILES!

24 hours a day, 7 days a week, 365 days a year, infectious disease experts are working to prevent and treat diseases caused by parasites.

IN THIS SECTION:

- ▶ how an entire family got infected with guinea worms;
- ▶ how a woman ended up with a worm in her brain;
- ▶ what was starting to eat away at a man's face.

These three case studies are true. However, names, places, and other details have been changed.

How do health-care workers get the job done?

Each of the cases you're about to read is very different. But the steps the health-care workers followed are similar. These health-care workers had to figure out—or diagnose—what's wrong with their patients. You can follow along with this process as you read the case studies. Keep an eye out for the icons below.

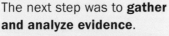

THE QUESTION At the beginning of each case, the health-care workers had **one or two main questions** they had to answer.

THE EVIDENCE The next step was to **gather and analyze evidence**. Health-care workers gather as much information as they can. Then they study it and figure out what it means.

THE CONCLUSION Along the way, workers come up with theories about what may have happened. They test these theories. Are the theories correct? **If so, the health-care workers have reached a conclusion**.

Ghana, West Africa
March 2006

One Family's Agony

A family in a small village in
Ghana has been infected with
guinea worm. The local
health-care worker tries
to figure out why.

Worm Invasion

Guinea worms return to a village in northern Ghana.

Kofi lives in a small village in Ghana, a country in Africa. It is his job to help control the guinea worm problem there. Every day, he visits people in the area and examines them for guinea worm.

Kofi had not found a guinea worm case in a year. Then one day in March 2006, he arrived at the home of the Fusheni family. Seven of the ten family members were seriously ill. The grandmother's feet were swollen with blisters. She couldn't collect wood for the fire. The parents were too weak to farm the fields. The two young children itched terribly. And the two older boys had open wounds on their legs. They had trouble walking, and they couldn't go to school.

Kofi knew right away that the Fushenis had guinea worm. But where did the worms come from? And why weren't any other villagers sick, too?

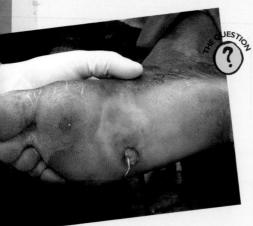

THE QUESTION (?)

A female guinea worm emerges from an infected person's foot. About 90% of the time, the guinea worms travel to their hosts' legs and feet. This makes walking extremely painful. The Fushenis, for example, found it impossible to work or go to school.

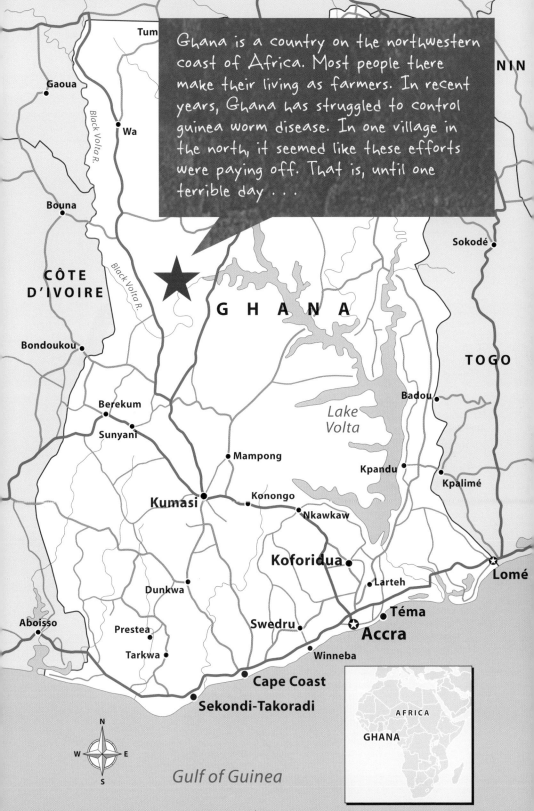

BURKINA FASO

Tum

Gaoua

Wa

Black Volta R.

NIN

Bouna

Sokodé

CÔTE
D'IVOIRE

Black Volta R.

G H A N A

TOGO

Bondoukou

Berekum

Badou

Lake
Volta

Sunyani

Mampong

Kpandu

Kpalimé

Kumasi

Konongo

Nkawkaw

Koforidua

Larteh

Lomé

Dunkwa

Téma

Aboisso

Swedru

Accra

Prestea

Winneba

Tarkwa

Cape Coast

Sekondi-Takoradi

AFRICA

GHANA

N

W   E

S

Gulf of Guinea

Ghana is a country on the northwestern coast of Africa. Most people there make their living as farmers. In recent years, Ghana has struggled to control guinea worm disease. In one village in the north, it seemed like these efforts were paying off. That is, until one terrible day . . .

LIFE OF THE GUINEA WORM
Here's how the guinea worm does its damage.

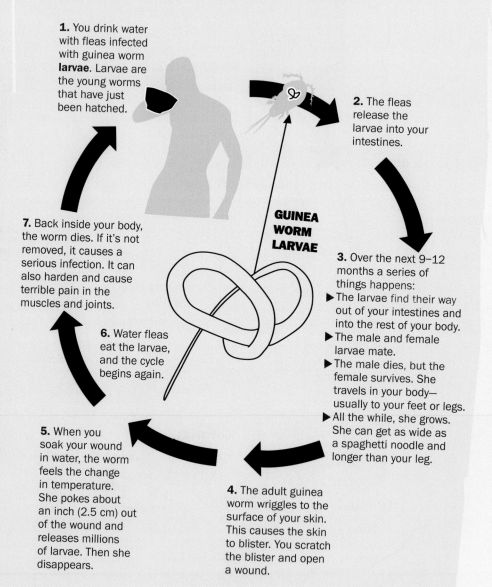

1. You drink water with fleas infected with guinea worm **larvae**. Larvae are the young worms that have just been hatched.

2. The fleas release the larvae into your intestines.

GUINEA WORM LARVAE

3. Over the next 9–12 months a series of things happens:
- ▶ The larvae find their way out of your intestines and into the rest of your body.
- ▶ The male and female larvae mate.
- ▶ The male dies, but the female survives. She travels in your body—usually to your feet or legs.
- ▶ All the while, she grows. She can get as wide as a spaghetti noodle and longer than your leg.

4. The adult guinea worm wriggles to the surface of your skin. This causes the skin to blister. You scratch the blister and open a wound.

5. When you soak your wound in water, the worm feels the change in temperature. She pokes about an inch (2.5 cm) out of the wound and releases millions of larvae. Then she disappears.

6. Water fleas eat the larvae, and the cycle begins again.

7. Back inside your body, the worm dies. If it's not removed, it causes a serious infection. It can also harden and cause terrible pain in the muscles and joints.

Detective Work

Can Kofi figure out where the Fushenis got the guinea worms?

Kofi sent for help from a medical team. The worms had to be removed, and the process can be slow, complicated, and painful.

In the meantime, Kofi needed to find out where the Fushenis became infected. He began by considering the facts.

Kofi already knew when the infection had happened. The worms were producing blisters. That meant the larvae—the young worms—had been growing for nine to 12 months. About a year before, the Fushenis must have drunk contaminated water.

But where did the water come from? There were three possibilities. First, the Fushenis could have been infected from a community water source. Second, they could have traveled somewhere else and drunk contaminated water. Third, they could have a private water source that had become contaminated.

Kofi knew that the first possibility was not likely. The village had been free of guinea worm for a year. If the local water were contaminated, other people would be infected.

Kofi then asked the family if they had traveled during the last year. None of them had left the village.

See pages 21–23 to find out how the worms are removed.

THE EVIDENCE

Here's a scene from a village in northern Ghana. Kofi was concerned about the Fushenis' entire village. He wanted to figure out how the family got the guinea worm—before other villagers became infected the same way.

Next, Kofi asked if the Fushenis had a private water source. At first he was told no. But Kofi didn't trust the answer. He kept repeating the question. And he explained how important the information was.

Finally, the grandmother admitted that they had a small pond on the farm. She said that the children liked to swim there. They also drank from the pond sometimes.

Kofi then asked the children about the pond. One of the boys remembered that a cousin had visited a year earlier. The cousin had a sore on his leg.

A young woman gathers water from a pond in Nigeria. The water must be filtered to remove the fleas that carry the guinea worm larvae.

Kofi had solved the mystery. Most likely, the cousin had guinea worm. When he swam in the pond, the worms released their larvae. The cousin went home, leaving his relatives with a dangerous present.

Luckily, the Fushenis had not used the community water source in the last year. The rest of the village was safe from infection.

Kofi turned his attention to treating the family.

The Treatment

The next weeks mean painful treatment for the Fushenis.

Removing a guinea worm takes time and a lot of patience. A team of health-care workers arrived to help Kofi. They worked carefully on each family member.

Kofi began by treating the oldest boy, Karim. Two of his worms were already hanging out of the sores. Kofi carefully cleaned the area around each of the wounds.

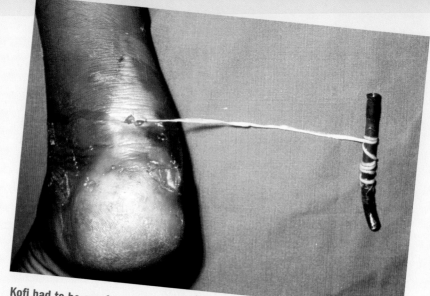

Kofi had to be careful as he removed a guinea worm. First, he pulled gently on it. Then, he wrapped it around a stick to keep it from going back into the patient's body. Next, he would return every few days to visit the patient and repeat this process.

Then he pulled gently on the end of a worm.

Little by little the worm began to come out. But Kofi knew not to force it. Guinea worms stretch like rubber bands. If Kofi pulled too hard, the worm would break. Most of it would shrink back into Karim's body. The worm would die and cause a bad infection.

Eventually, Kofi felt that the worm would not come out any farther. So he took a tiny piece of a twig from a tree. He wrapped the exposed part of the worm around the twig over and over. Then he taped the stick to Karim's leg so the worm would not unwind.

Kofi did the same thing with Karim's other worm. Then, Kofi bandaged the wounds to

TRACKING THE WORM

The Carter Center provides special medical kits to volunteers working to prevent and treat guinea worm. Here's what these kits contain.

gloves: worn to protect health-care workers and patients from each other's germs

gauze packets: cloth and tape to cover wounds

topical ointment: to place on wounds to avoid additional infection

surveillance log: for the volunteer to record all guinea worm activity

small wooden sticks: used to wrap the worms around

This young person in Togo is having a guinea worm removed. The removal process is often long and painful. Sometimes a guinea worm can be pulled out in a few days. But often it takes weeks.

keep them clean and hold the worms in place. He promised to return in two days.

While the Fushenis waited, guinea worms still floated in their pond. It was time to get rid of them before they found another host.

Cleaning Up

Kofi and his team chase the rest of the worms out of the village.

Every two days, the health-care workers went back to visit the Fushenis. Each time, they worked carefully on the worms. Slowly, they made progress.

In the meantime, Kofi found the Fushenis' pond. He estimated how much water it contained. He carefully measured out the right amount of a poison called **ABATE**. Then he poured it into the pond. Within six hours, the guinea worms and water fleas in the pond were dead. The water was once again safe to drink.

ABATE is just one of the weapons African countries are using against guinea worms. Many villages now have filters to strain fleas from their drinking water. Public health workers also give **pipe filters** to children. Pipe filters are hard plastic straws with a screen at the bottom end. Children wear them around their necks so they can drink filtered water.

Had Karim had a pipe filter, he might have avoided a lot of trouble. His worms had wrapped themselves around tendons and muscles in his legs. Simply taking a step caused terrible pain.

This Ghanaian boy is drinking water through a pipe filter. This pipe filters out the small fleas that are host to the guinea worm—and prevents the boy from being infected.

Volunteers at the Carter Center are assembling kits that will help health-care workers prevent and treat guinea worm disease.

It took three weeks for Kofi to remove the first worm from Karim's leg. It was almost four feet (1.2 m) long.

Kofi and his team worked with the Fushenis for two months. In the end, the seven infected family members recovered. Between them, they had hosted a total of 26 worms.

After he recovered, Karim was grateful. He decided to help others learn from his experience. He now travels to other villages to tell people about guinea worm. He warns people to filter their water. He even carries a pipe filter to make sure other children don't make the same mistake he did. **24/7**

Volunteers like Karim speak directly to children and adults. Here, a volunteer is teaching Ghanaian children how to avoid the guinea worm—and what to do if they're infected.

Aryc W. Mosher works for the Carter Center's Guinea Worm Eradication Program. Here, he talks about the disease.

24/7: Why are guinea worms so hard to treat?

ARYC W. MOSHER: No medication can kill the worm once it is inside of you. And there is no medication that prevents you from getting the worm.

24/7: Can the worm be coaxed out?

MOSHER: You can fool the worm by getting a large bucket of water and putting the infected part in it. This brings the worm out to release its larvae. The water also helps to lubricate the worm, making it easier to pull it out.

24/7: What happens once the worm is wound around a stick?

MOSHER: It stays alive for a while. But worms need to keep wet to live. The part on the stick begins to dry. That makes it harder for the worm to pull itself back into the body.

24/7: What if the worm isn't removed?

MOSHER: Shortly after the worm releases its larvae, it dies. If it's not removed, it causes major infections. Some worms that never reach the skin's surface turn hard. It is as if they turn into hard sticks inside the body.

In the next case, a medical team tries to figure out if a parasite is making a woman unable to talk.

Simi Valley,
California
December 26, 1990

The Case of the Trespassing Tapeworm

Something is dramatically affecting
Danielle Jordan's brain. But her doctors
can't figure out what it is.

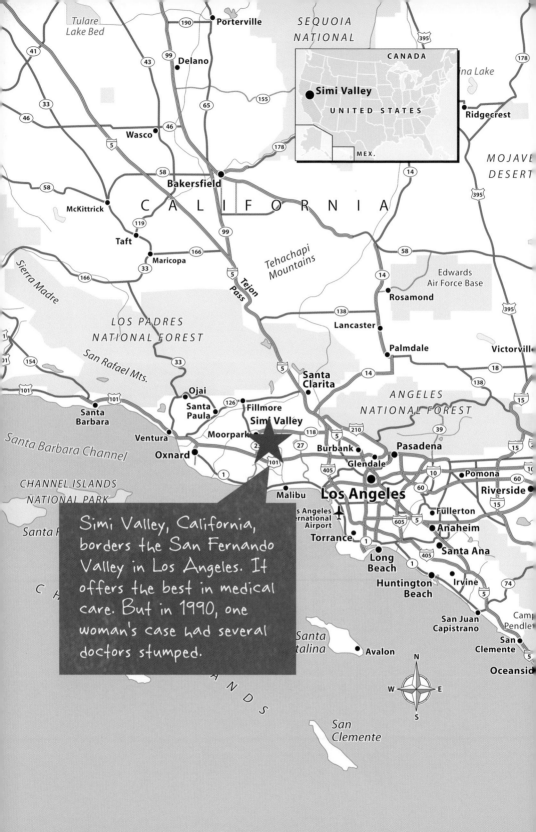

Simi Valley, California, borders the San Fernando Valley in Los Angeles. It offers the best in medical care. But in 1990, one woman's case had several doctors stumped.

"Call My Parents!"

What happens when a talkative woman suddenly can't speak?

Danielle Jordan designed ads for phone books. She often visited clients to discuss their ads. Jordan liked that part of her job. She was outgoing and loved to talk—until one day, when she couldn't say a word.

On December 26, 1990, Jordan went to visit the owner of a flower shop. The two were talking, when suddenly Jordan stopped in the middle of a sentence. She couldn't finish her thought. She knew what she wanted to say, but the words would not come out.

Her client stared at her, trying to figure out what was wrong. Jordan grabbed a piece of paper and wrote, "Call my parents." She scribbled down their phone number.

By the time her parents arrived, Jordan was talking again. But the right side of her face was twitching. Her parents took her to a nearby medical clinic.

Danielle Jordan was in the middle of a conversation with a client. Then, suddenly, she couldn't speak. She wrote a note, asking the client for help.

Rushed to the Hospital

Jordan needs more help than a clinic can provide.

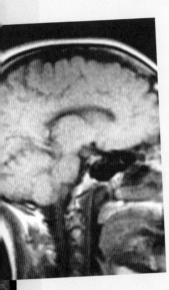

An MRI gives a detailed view of the brain. According to Dr. Soudmand, a CT scan of Jordan's brain showed a lesion on her brain. He then ordered an MRI to confirm this diagnosis. The MRI also showed what the doctor thought was a tumor—possibly cancer.

A few hours later, Jordan sat with Dr. Rasoul Soudmand at the hospital. Dr. Soudmand had the results of Jordan's **CT scan**. That's a high-powered **x-ray**. "The news is bad," the doctor told Jordan. She had a small lesion, or injury, in her brain that appeared to be a **tumor**. The lesion was located near the part of the brain that controls speech. It was causing her speech difficulties. It was also causing seizures, which are sudden attacks in the brain.

"Most likely," Dr. Soudmand told Jordan, "you will need surgery."

A Different Diagnosis

Jordan gets other doctors involved.

Jordan went home to her husband and her 11-year-old son. Together, they decided to get other opinions on her condition.

She went to see a friend of a friend named Dr. Leslie Cahan.

Dr. Cahan studied Jordan's x-rays. After a long pause he said, "I don't see a tumor." Instead, Dr. Cahan saw a worm.

Usually, tapeworms like this one live in the intestines and steal nutrients from their host. But in rare cases, they end up in other parts of the body, like the brain. That's what happened to Danielle Jordan.

The pea-shaped thing in Jordan's brain was a parasite called a tapeworm, he said. Usually tapeworms live in the intestines.

But sometimes tapeworms escape the intestines. They can find their way into the central nervous system or the brain.

Was a tapeworm really lodged in Jordan's brain? If so, where did she get it? And how could she get rid of it?

THE QUESTION **?**

LIFE OF THE PORK TAPEWORM
Here's how the worm does its damage.

2. The eggs hatch in the pig's intestine.

3. The worms travel to the pig's muscles, and possibly the brain and liver.

4. The adult worms lay eggs in the pig's intestines.

5. The pig produces manure, which contains tapeworm eggs.

To You . . .
6. You eat pork that has not been well cooked and consume a tapeworm egg.

7. Or you drink water contaminated with manure from an infected pig. Or you eat food washed in contaminated water.

8. The tapeworm eggs hatch in your intestines.

From the pig . . .
1. A pig eats something with tapeworm eggs in it.

9. The worms travel to your muscles, and possibly to your brain and liver.

31

Tracking the Tapeworm

Where did Jordan get the tapeworm?

Danielle Jordan met next with Dr. Pamela Nagami. Dr. Nagami specializes in infectious diseases. In her book *The Woman with a Worm in Her Head*, she described the case.

First, Dr. Nagami recalled, she ordered a spinal tap. A test on Jordan's spinal fluid would determine whether she had a tapeworm. Then, Dr. Nagami began asking questions.

Dr. Nagami asked Jordan where she ate. People usually get tapeworms from eating poorly cooked pork or beef. She also asked Jordan where she had traveled. In many countries, parasites are common in the water supply.

Six years earlier, Jordan had visited Puerto Vallarta, Mexico. "We went to a famous restaurant where all the movie stars go," she recalled. "That day I did something I would have never done ordinarily. I ordered a salad."

Dr. Nagami thought she had found the answer. The lettuce in Jordan's salad may have been washed with contaminated tap water. Or people in the kitchen may have had tapeworm. If they failed to wash their hands, they could have passed the tapeworm larvae on to Danielle through her food.

Jordan may have gotten the tapeworm here, in Puerto Vallarta. That's a popular vacation spot in Mexico. "Chances are you've been harboring this worm for at least six years," Dr. Nagami told Jordan.

Before long, the test results came in with yet another answer. There were signs of tapeworm in Jordan's spinal fluid.

"Chances are you've been harboring this worm for at least six years," Dr. Nagami told Jordan.

Worm Killer

Dr. Nagami goes after the worm.

After meeting with Dr. Nagami, Danielle Jordan entered the hospital for the treatment. The medication used to kill the worm was dangerous. The doctors wanted to watch over her.

On the first day, Jordan had no problems. On the second day, she had a headache and a low fever. Doctors guessed that the worm was reacting to the medication. After more than two weeks of treatment, the doctors declared that the worm had died.

More than two years later, Danielle Jordan had another **MRI**. All it showed was a very tiny abnormality. Dr. Nagami called this abnormality, "a souvenir of her encounter with the worm." 24/7

Dr. Pamela Nagami talks about the world of parasites.

24/7: Why did doctors first believe Danielle Jordon had a brain tumor and not a worm?

DR. PAMELA NAGAMI: Danielle does not eat pork because of her religion. Everybody thought she had a brain tumor because she had seizures. But it's important to know that the pork tapeworm is the most common cause of seizures worldwide.

24/7: If Jordon doesn't eat pork, then how did she get the tapeworm?

NAGAMI: The pork tapeworm lives in a human being and that person passes the worm's eggs. It just takes one egg. In Danielle's case, she ate a salad, which most likely was contaminated with [a tapeworm] egg. This egg got into Danielle's bloodstream and then lodged in her brain.

24/7: Do most of us have parasites living in our bodies?

NAGAMI: Not really, because most of us live in a modern society with a sewage system. But in nature, all animals have parasites.

In the next case, a patient hopes that a parasite doesn't eat him alive!

San Fernando Valley
Hospital, California
February 1, 2003

What's Eating His Face?

Doctors find mysterious
bumps on a paticnt's
chin. Will they be able to
find out what's eating
this man's face?

Strange Bumps

Alfred Eliah has sores on his chin. And they're leaking yellow stuff.

It was the middle of January. Alfred Eliah was inspecting the swollen bumps underneath his chin. He first broke out with the bumps in December. Now they were getting worse.

Eliah and his wife, Helene, had recently returned from a trip to the Tambopata Candano National Reserve in Peru. They had volunteered to help a team of **biologists** study birds in the area.

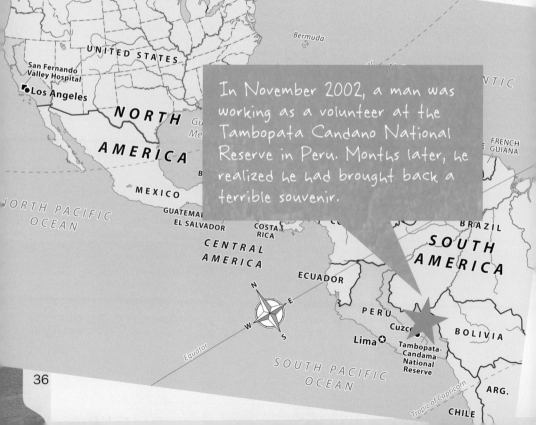

In November 2002, a man was working as a volunteer at the Tambopata Candano National Reserve in Peru. Months later, he realized he had brought back a terrible souvenir.

Eliah recalled that one of the guides at the reserve had similar bumps on his arm. The guide had told them it was from **leishmaniasis**. This disease comes from a tiny parasite that travels in a very small insect called a sand fly. A bite from a sand fly can pass on the parasite.

And the parasite, once in a human's system, may attack the nose and mouth area, and literally eat it away.

As days passed, Eliah kept an eye on the lesions. They were firm and growing larger. By February 2003, they started oozing a yellow fluid. Eliah was worried. "We'd better get to a hospital," he told Helene.

Sand flies pass on the parasite that causes leishmaniasis. Alfred Eliah was exposed to these dangerous pests in Peru.

LIFE OF THE SAND FLY

Here's how the sand fly passes on leishmaniasis.

1. The female sand fly that is host to a parasite bites you. She injects a young form of the parasite into your blood.

2. The parasite reproduces in your body.

3. Another sand fly bites you and takes a meal of blood. It absorbs the parasite and flies off for another blood meal.

Stumped by Bumps

Eliah goes to see a doctor. A specialist is called in.

Eliah went to a walk-in clinic in San Fernando Valley, California. He told the physician on duty about his recent trip to Peru, and his suspicion that he had leishmaniasis.

The doctor immediately called infectious disease specialist Dr. Pamela Nagami. "I've got a 72-year-old guy down here that was in the jungle in Peru and now has a weird ulcer," he told her. "He says he thinks it might be leishmaniasis."

It was Dr. Nagami's job to determine if Eliah had this parasite-borne disease.

"I had never seen a case of leishmaniasis," recalls Dr. Nagami in her book *Bitten*. "But I knew that the American form, untreated, could eat up the middle of a person's face, starting with the nose. The Portuguese in Brazil call the condition *espundia*, or sponge. That's what the patient's face becomes—a ragged, porous hole, like a sea sponge."

Dr. Nagami started her investigation.

She arrived at the hospital and inspected Eliah's sores. They were the size of nickels. Each had a scab in the center and pink around the edges. "I need to check with

The CDC is a government agency. Among its many duties, it works to prevent and control infectious and chronic diseases.

some leishmaniasis specialists to find out our next steps," Dr. Nagami told Eliah.

Dr. Nagami contacted an expert at the **CDC** in Atlanta. His name was Frank Steurer. He worked in the branch of the CDC specializing in parasites.

Steurer promised Dr. Nagami that he'd send her a special kit for **specimens** from Eliah's lesions.

Two days later, the kit arrived in a cardboard-and-metal tube marked with an orange biohazard label. It held two screw-top plastic tubes for Eliah's specimens.

For the first specimen, a skin doctor removed a piece of the sore. For the second, a disease specialist stuck a needle into one of Eliah's lesions and removed some pus.

Dr. Nagami put the specimens in the tubes and shipped the package back to the CDC.

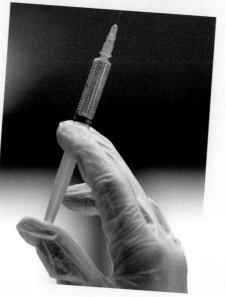

Doctors used a needle to remove a sample of pus from Alfred Eliah's lesions. The CDC then tested the pus to figure out what had caused the infection.

SAVING FACE

Want to avoid leishmaniasis? Of course you do. Here's some advice.

There are no vaccines to protect against leishmaniasis. If you're traveling to an area where sand flies exist, the CDC recommends the following:

▶ Stay in rooms with screens on the windows or air-conditioned areas.

▶ Avoid going out from dusk to dawn, when sand flies are most active.

▶ Wear long-sleeve shirts, pants, and socks.

▶ Wear insect repellent on uncovered skin and under the ends of sleeves or pants.

▶ Spray clothing and sleeping areas with an insecticide to kill insects.

Treatment Torture

It's not easy getting Eliah the right medicine. And it's not easy taking it, either.

Forty-eight hours later, Dr. Nagami received a call from Frank Steurer at the CDC. Eliah's specimens had tested positive for leishmaniasis.

Dr. Nagami knew that a drug called Pentostam offered Eliah the best chance for a cure. There were several problems with the drug, however.

First, Pentostam had not yet been approved by the U.S. Food and Drug Administration

(**FDA**). Dr. Nagami was persistent, though, and got special permission to use the drug for 20 days.

The second problem was more complicated. Eliah was 72 years old and had a history of heart problems. And Pentostam could be very dangerous. It could cause severe muscle and joint aches, vomiting, and problems with internal organs.

Dr. Nagami turned to Eliah's heart doctor for advice. The **cardiologist**, Dr. Jocelyn Turnier, advised that Eliah be closely monitored as he took the drug. By his second week, Eliah was getting tired. He had bad headaches and pain in his muscles.

Would the treatment kill him?

Leishmaniasis is found in parts of about 88 countries. Here, a 23-year-old soldier from Colombia shows leishmaniasis sores on his arm. He got the disease while on patrol in the jungles in the southern part of the country.

Case Closed

Eliah's treatments are complete.

Dr. Nagami and Eliah's other doctors determined that he could continue taking the medication.

Eventually, his lesions started to heal. A scab that had been on the inside of one eye even slid out one day.

Eliah had e-mailed the volunteers from Peru and told them about his illness. He later found out that his e-mail had caught the attention of another person from the trip. A young filmmaker had a lesion on his arm. When he received Eliah's e-mail, he had it checked. He, too, had leishmaniasis, but recovered after taking Pentostam.

The trip to Peru had been all about studying birds. But for Eliah, it was the tiny parasite inside a sand fly that had left the most powerful memories. **24/7**

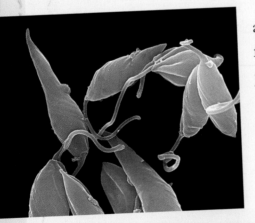

This is an enlarged image of the parasite that causes leishmaniasis.

MEDICAL

DOWNLOAD

Here's even more amazing stuff about parasites for you to ingest.

IN THIS SECTION:

▶ where parasites have popped up in the past;

▶ how parasitic diseases have been in the news;

▶ the tools and equipment that are used to study and treat parasites;

▶ and whether being an infectious disease doctor might be in your future!

1400s B.C. Ancient Worms

The guinea worm parasite appears in Egyptian medical texts. The worm is referred to as a "fiery serpent" because of the way it causes a burning sensation when it emerges from a human's skin.

See "One Family's Agony" on page 15.

1300s The Plague

The bubonic plague infects people in Europe, Africa, and the Middle East. Also called the Black Death, the deadly disease (*below*) is caused by a parasite that is spread through fleabites. In Europe alone, the plague kills at least 20 million people.

Key Dates in the History of

1936 What About Baseball Cards?

The U.S. Department of Agriculture begins housing a collection of parasites in a converted farm in Maryland. Today, this National Parasite Collection is one of the three largest in the world. Why collect parasites? So researchers in the future can study them and find out how they spread to humans and animals.

1991 Parasites on Ice

The well-preserved body of a 5,000-year-old man (*below left*) is discovered in a glacier in the Austrian Alps. Inside his stomach, researchers find samples of bread, plants, and meat. But most astoundingly, they pull a roundworm parasite from his intestines!

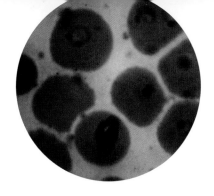

1673 Up Close and Personal

In the Netherlands, Anton van Leeuwenhoek becomes the first person actually to see parasites.

This Dutch shopkeeper and amateur scientist creates a microscope that allows him to see parasites in drops of rainwater. He then studies other specimens—like scrapings from his teeth and his own waste. He concludes that the human body is host to countless parasites.

1878–1882 Deadly Bites

Alphonse Laveran, a French doctor and scientist, traces **malaria** to its source. He discovers that the disease is caused by a parasite that is transferred to humans by mosquito bites. Previously, people believed that the disease came from bad air. (In Italian, *mala* means "bad," and *aria* means "air.")

Parasites

Parasites have been making pests of themselves throughout history.

2006 A President's Promise

Former U.S. president Jimmy Carter (*right*) makes a bold announcement: Guinea worm is soon to become the next disease after smallpox to be wiped off the face of the Earth. Carter and his wife, Rosalynn Carter, started the Carter Center in 1982. Among the center's many goals is to combat many diseases caused by parasites.

In the News

Read all about it! Diseases caused by parasites are front-page news.

Gates Foundation Attacks Parasites!

SEATTLE, WASHINGTON—September 15, 2006

Bill Gates is famous for being the richest person on earth. He helped to found the software company Microsoft and is worth about $53 billion. But he would also like to be known for other accomplishments.

In 2000, Bill Gates and his wife, Melinda, formed the Bill and Melinda Gates Foundation. Their aim is to improve health care and education around the world.

In 2006, the foundation made an announcement. They were giving money to help research neglected tropical diseases.

Diseases like **hookworm** and leishmaniasis are transmitted by parasites and worms. They affect hundreds of millions of people each year in Latin America, Asia, and Africa. And currently no vaccines exist to prevent them.

Tachi Yamada works for the Gates Foundation. She told *Medical News Today*, "Many of the world's [worst] illnesses are virtually unheard of in the rich world. But they're a fact of life for millions of people in poor countries."

Melinda and Bill Gates (*the couple in the center*) visit a malaria research hospital in Mozambique in 2003. Their foundation has given $158 million to fight this parasitic disease.

Rosalynn Carter greets a group of people in a village in Ghana. Carter and her husband, former U.S. president Jimmy Carter, traveled to the country in 2007 to help with efforts to eradicate guinea worm disease.

Carter Foundation Receives Award

ATLANTA, GEORGIA—May 15, 2006

The Carter Center received the 2006 Gates Award for Global Health from the Bill and Melinda Gates Foundation. The center was recognized for its work in the fight against neglected diseases.

The Carter Center was founded in 1982 by former U.S. president Jimmy Carter and his wife, Rosalynn Carter.

In 1986, the center began a program to combat guinea worm disease. The guinea worm is a parasite that grows in the human body and causes intense pain and damage. In 1986, there were about 3.5 million cases of the disease. In 2005, there were fewer than 11,000 cases.

The Carter Center has also worked to combat river blindness. That's a disease caused by parasitic worms. It causes terrible sores and even blindness. It affects nearly 17 million people.

Biological Hazards

Have a look at the tools and equipment used by infectious disease specialists.

TOOLS AND EQUIPMENT

microscope Used to see tiny details that can't be viewed with the eye alone.

syringe Used for giving injections and for taking blood. It is a tube with a plunger and a hollow needle attached.

slides Small, thin pieces of glass. Technicians smear specimens on them and examine the specimens under a microscope.

MRI machine These are used to create views of the inside of the human body. MRI scans enable experts to diagnose many diseases and injuries. *MRI* stands for *magnetic resonance imaging*.

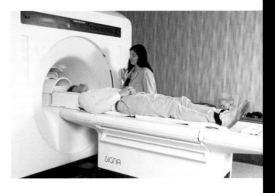

CT This test uses special x-ray equipment to create images of different types of tissue. *CT* stands for *computerized tomography* and it is often referred to as a CAT scan.

x-ray machine A device that uses beams of light to take pictures of teeth, bones, and organs inside the body.

PROTECTIVE GEAR

goggles Protects workers' eyes from blood and body fluids.

scrub suits The basic uniforms of doctors and nurses. Prevents health-care workers from transferring germs and disease.

facemask Protects workers' eyes, nose, and mouth; protects patients from germs and disease.

plastic aprons Protect health-care workers from blood and other body fluids.

gloves Protect workers' hands from disease; protects patients from germs and disease.

49

HELP WANTED: Infectious Disease Doctor

Are you finding that an interest in contagious diseases is catching? Here's more information.

Q&A: DR. PAMELA NAGAMI

24/7: How would you describe your job?

DR. PAMELA NAGAMI: It's similar to being an investigator. What I do with my patients is I look for clues. I like biology and I like to learn about different organisms. It just happens that the organisms I study eat people alive.

24/7: Is there a lot of pressure at work?

NAGAMI: Yes. I make a lot of life-and-death decisions. You have to think fast and be decisive. It's always challenging, but the key to being a doctor is to control your feelings. You stay calm in the face of disaster.

24/7: Are you ever worried about getting sick?

NAGAMI: Infectious disease doctors do get exposed to a lot. For instance, with a meningococcal sepsis case, it's **toxic** just being in the same room with them. It can kill you in 12 hours.

24/7: With your hectic schedule, do you have time for your own family?

NAGAMI: I've been married 25 years and I've got two grown kids. I managed to do it all.

A Day in the Life

Dr. Nagami shares with the writer a typical day.

Dr. Pamela Nagami is an infectious disease doctor in Los Angeles, California.

From: Nagami, Pamela H
To: TommiLewisTilden
Re: Parasite manuscript
Sent: Wednesday, February 08, 2006, 4:35 P.M.

This morning I sent my patient home to finish recovering from an **abscess**.

Consulted on a patient with two ulcers on her ankle down to the bone (mysterious case as she is only 39).

Saw a woman with a lesion on her lip and an odd painful rash on her fingers and toes. I walked her down to see the **dermatologist**.

Consulted with the surgeon on an 83-year-old with a gaping, non-healing abdominal incision.

Consulted with another surgeon on a man with both legs **amputated** below the knee that needs one leg off above the knee due to an aggressive infection. But he's refusing to do the amputation. (He may die.)

Tried to figure out what kind of infection is eating up the tendons on my hospitalized patient with the hand and arm infection.

Arranged for a man who found out yesterday he was HIV positive to see our social worker.

And the day is still young!

From: Nagami, Pamela H
To: TommiLewisTilden
Re: Update
Sent: Thursday, February 09, 2006, 2:19 P.M.

P.S.
The guy is agreeing to the amputation.

MEDICAL DOWNLOAD

CAREERS

HELP WANTED:
Communications Director

You don't have to be a doctor or scientist to help fight infectious diseases.

Q&A: ARYC W. MOSHER

Aryc W. Mosher works in public health. He is the assistant director for the Carter Center's Guinea Worm Eradication Program.

24/7: What kind of education do you have?

ARYC W. MOSHER: I have a degree in communication arts and sciences. I also have a master's degree in public health in epidemiology (the study of diseases).

24/7: How did you get interested in public health?

MOSHER: I was always interested in developing messages to help change people. After college, I signed up with the Peace Corps. I went to Africa to work for three and a half years on AIDS and HIV prevention. Years later, I ended up in Ghana working as an adviser to the National Guinea Worm Eradication Program.

24/7: What did you do in Ghana?

MOSHER: I managed money and developed proposals for the guinea worm program. I also attended ceremonies and met with village chiefs. Sometimes villages did not want to have a chemical (ABATE) put into their water source. They'd hear that it'd make them sick or **sterile** or kill the fish. So I'd go in with a team and talk to the chief and convince them it was safe.

24/7: What was the most memorable case you worked on?

MOSHER: A young boy, maybe 12 years old, who biked about 25 miles (40 km) to our office to have his guinea worms treated. It was quite a physical act. Here was a young person wanting to get control of his situation and determined to do something about it.

THE STATS

DAY JOB: Many infectious disease doctors work as primary care physicians, at universities, or in health offices.

MONEY: The average salary for an infectious disease doctor is $185,920.

EDUCATION: Infectious disease doctors must finish the following:
▶ 4 years of college;
▶ 4 years of medical school;
▶ 3 or more years training with a doctor;
▶ 2–3 years of specialized training in infectious diseases.

THE NUMBERS: There are at least 8,000 infectious disease doctors in the United States.

24/7: Any suggestions for someone who wants to have a career in public health?

MOSHER: You can volunteer at hospitals or work for public health campaigns. Like the anti-smoking campaign, for example. Think of anything that helps people live healthier lives. In college, you can take classes in health communications and health promotions.

If you want to travel and get public health experience overseas, go online and check out organizations like the Peace Corps or Project Hope. There are lots of opportunities to see the world, gain experience in health issues, and make a difference in people's lives.

DO YOU HAVE WHAT IT TAKES?

Take this totally unscientific quiz to find out if being an infectious disease doctor might be a good career for you.

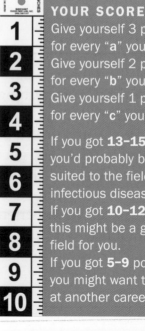

1 **How do you feel about school?**
a) I love school and studying and could do it for years.
b) I'm happy to get as much education as I need to meet my goals.
c) I'd like to stop going to school after I graduate from college.

2 **When I'm faced with something I don't understand, I:**
a) ask questions, study books, and search the Internet.
b) ask my friends.
c) pretend I know what's going on.

3 **How are you when meeting new people?**
a) I like new people and try to make them feel comfortable.
b) I like new people but sometimes don't know what to say to them.
c) I don't like meeting new people.

4 **Are you interested in solving medical problems?**
a) Yes. I want to be a doctor.
b) Sometimes. I like to watch medical shows on TV.
c) No, that's not my thing.

5 **Do you get grossed out easily?**
a) Never. I like to watch operations on TV.
b) I don't mind the sight of my own blood.
c) I feel sick just thinking about a paper cut.

YOUR SCORE

Give yourself 3 points for every "**a**" you chose. Give yourself 2 points for every "**b**" you chose. Give yourself 1 point for every "**c**" you chose.

If you got **13–15** points, you'd probably be well suited to the field of infectious disease.

If you got **10–12** points, this might be a good field for you.

If you got **5–9** points, you might want to look at another career.

54

HOW TO GET STARTED . . . NOW!

It's never too early to start working toward your goals.

GET AN EDUCATION

▶ Starting now, take as many biology, chemistry, physics, health, and math classes as you can. Train yourself to ask questions, gather new information, and make conclusions the way infectious disease specialists do.

▶ Work on your communication skills. Join the drama club or debate team. It's good practice in thinking before you speak and listening to others.

▶ Start thinking about college. Look for ones that have good science programs. Call or write to those colleges to get information.

▶ Read the newspapers. Keep up with what's happening in your community.

▶ Read about infectious diseases. Learn about historical and recent cases. See the books and Web sites in the Resources section on pages 56–58.

▶ Graduate from high school!

NETWORK!

Ask your own doctor for advice about becoming an infectious disease specialist.

Get in touch with your local hospital. Ask if you can interview an infectious disease doctor. Maybe spend a day with him or her to get a sense of what they do.

GET AN INTERNSHIP

Call your local hospital or doctor's offices. There might be internships available. It doesn't hurt to ask!

LEARN ABOUT OTHER JOBS IN THE FIELD!

There are other jobs in infectious diseases besides being an infectious disease specialist. Here are some of them.

parasitologist: studies parasites

biologist: studies living organisms

microbiologist: studies microscopic cells in human illnesses

zoologist: specializes in animal life

pathologist: studies disease, especially its effects on body tissue

entomologist: specializes in insects

ecologist: studies how organisms relate to the environment

epidemiologist: studies what causes, and how to control, epidemics

infectious disease pharmacist: dispenses infectious disease medication

55

Resources

Looking for more information about parasites and infectious diseases? Here are some resources you won't want to miss!

PROFESSIONAL ORGANIZATIONS

Centers for Disease Control and Prevention (CDC)
www.cdc.gov
1600 Clifton Road
Atlanta, GA 30333
PHONE: 800-311-3435

The CDC was founded in 1946, primarily to fight malaria. It is part of the Department of Health and Human Services. Today, the group is a leader in efforts to prevent and control disease, injuries, workplace hazards, and environmental and health threats.

Infectious Diseases Society of America (IDSA)
www.idsociety.org
66 Canal Center Plaza, Suite 600
Alexandria, VA 22324
PHONE: 703-299-0200
FAX: 703-299-0204
E-MAIL: info@idsociety.org

The IDSA represents physicians, scientists, and other health-care professionals who specialize in infectious diseases. The society's purpose is to improve the health of individuals, communities, and society by promoting excellence in patient care, education, research, public health, and prevention relating to infectious diseases.

International Society for Infectious Diseases (ISID)

www.isid.org
1330 Beacon Street, Suite 228
Brookline, MA 02446
PHONE: 617-277-0551
FAX: 617-278-9113
E-MAIL: info@isid.org

The ISID is committed to improving the care of patients with infectious diseases, the training of clinicians and researchers in infectious diseases and microbiology, and the control of infectious diseases around the world.

National Institute of Allergy and Infectious Diseases (NIAID)

www3.niaid.nih.gov
6610 Rockledge Drive, MSC 612
Bethesda, MD 20892
PHONE: 301-496-5717

For more than 50 years, NIAID has conducted research that helps treat, prevent, and better understand infectious and other diseases. It is part of the National Institutes of Health.

Society of Infectious Disease Pharmacists (SIDP)

www.sidp.org
823 Congress Avenue, Suite 230
Austin, TX 78701
PHONE: 512-479-0425
FAX: 512-495-9031
E-MAIL: sidp@eami.com

The SIDP provides education, advocacy, and leadership in all aspects of the treatment of infectious diseases. The society is comprised of pharmacists and other health-care professionals involved in patient care, research, teaching, drug development, and governmental regulation.

WEB SITES

National Center for Infectious Diseases
www.cdc.gov/ncidod/id_links.htm
Planning to travel to a foreign country? Check out this site to learn how to avoid getting an infectious disease.

National Library of Medicine
www.medlineplus.gov
This is the largest medical library in the world. It has information about studies being done on infectious diseases.

***Science* Magazine Online**
www.sciencemag.org
Check out their archives for cool articles and photos on parasites.

U.S. Department of Agriculture
www.ars.usda.gov
Look here for updated information about food safety.

World Health Organization
www.who.int/en/
This international organization offers infectious disease information in English, French, and Spanish.

BOOKS FOR YOUNG READERS

Facklam, Howard and Margery. *Parasites* (Invaders). New York: Twenty-First Century Books, 1997.

Fleischer, Paul. *Parasites: Latching on to a Free Lunch* (Discovery). New York: Twenty-First Century Books, 2006.

Fredericks, Anthony. *Bloodsucking Creatures*. Danbury, Conn.: Franklin Watts, 2003.

Harrison, Paul. *Micro Bugs* (Up Close). New York: Rosen Publishing, 2007.

Houston, Rob. *Feeders* (Parasites and Partners). Austin: Raintree, 2003.

Martin, James W. *Killers* (Parasites and Partners). Austin: Raintree, 2003.

Viegas, Jennifer. *Parasites* (Germs! The Library of Disease-Causing Organisms). New York: Rosen Publishing, 2004.

BOOKS BY DR. NAGAMI

Bitten: True Medical Stories of Bites and Stings. New York: St. Martin's Griffin, 2005.

The Woman with the Worm in Her Head: And Other True Stories of Infectious Disease. New York: St. Martin's Griffin, 2002.

A

ABATE (uh-BAYT) *noun* a special solution that is used to contain an area, usually water, and kills parasites living in the area

abscess (AB-ses) *noun* pus around an inflamed area

amputated (AM-pyoo-tate-id) *verb* cut off

B

biologists (bye-OL-uh-jists) *noun* scientists who study living organisms

blood test (blud test) *noun* a blood sample taken from a patient, either by poking a finger or placing a needle in a vein, so the doctor can study it and determine if there are organisms in the patient's blood and body

C

cardiologist (kar-dee-OHL-uh-jist) *noun* a doctor who specializes in heart disease and treatment

CDC (see-dee-SEE) *noun* a government agency in charge of protecting public health. It is short for the *Centers for Disease Control and Prevention.*

contaminated (kuhn-TAM-uh-nay-tid) *adjective* describing something that has been made dirty or unfit for use, as in *contaminated drinking water*

CT scan (SEE-tee SKAN) *noun* a device that uses x-rays to look inside the body; also called a CAT scan. It's short for *computerized tomography.*

D

dermatologist (dur-ma-TOHL-uh-jist) *noun* a doctor who specializes in skin problems

diagnose (dye-uhg-NOHSS) *verb* to find or identify a disease

dracunculiasis (dra-kun-kuh-LYE-uh-sis) *noun* an infection caused by a worm that comes from water fleas. Also known as guinea worm disease.

E

eradicate (ih-RAD-uh-kate) *verb* to remove or eliminate

Dictionary

F

FDA (ef-dee-AYE) *noun* a government agency that monitors the food supply and evaluates medications for use. It is short for the *U.S. Food and Drug Administration*.

H

hookworm (HOOK-wurm) *noun* a parasitic worm with hook-like mouth parts that attach to the inside of a host's intestinal wall

host organism (hohst OR-guh-niz-uhm) *noun* any life-form—like a plant or animal—where a parasite lives

I

infection (in-FEK-shun) *noun* the condition when a body part in invaded with a disease

infectious disease doctor (in-FEK-shuhss duh-ZEEZ DOK-tur) *noun* a medical doctor who is an expert in diseases caused by bacteria, parasites, viruses, and fungi

internal medicine doctors (in-TUR-nuhl MED-uh-suhn DOK-terz) *noun* the first doctors you see in a medical office. They analyze your condition and sometimes consult or refer you to specialists.

L

larvae (LAR-vee) *noun* newly hatched insects or parasites. The singular is larva.

leishmaniasis (leesh-mah-NYE-uh-sis) *noun* an infection caused by a worm that comes from sand flies

lesions (LEE-zhenz) *noun* abnormalities in skin tissue, such as boils or rashes; can also appear internally, for instance, in the brain

M

malaria (ma-LAIR-e-a) *noun* a serious infection transmitted by a mosquito bite

microscopic (mye-kruh-SKOP-ik) *adjective* describing something so small it can only be seen under a microscope

MRI (em-ahr-EYE) *noun* a test that produces computerized images of a patient's body. It's short for *magnetic resonance imaging*.

N

neurologists (nur-OHL-uh-jists) *noun* doctors who treat the brain and nervous system

P

parasite (PAH-ruh-site) *noun* an organism that lives on, or in, another host or carrier. Parasites need a living host (human, plant, animal) in order to get food and survive.

pathologist (pah-THOL-uh-jist) *noun* a doctor who analyzes blood to help diagnose disease

pipe filters (pipe FILL-terz) *noun* devices used to filter parasites from drinking water

pus (puhs) *noun* a thick yellowish-white fluid that forms in infected tissue and contains bacteria

R

radiologists (ra-dee-OHL-uh-jists) *noun* doctors who specialize in taking and reading x-rays and other forms of imaging techniques

S

seizures (see-zhurz) *noun* sudden contractions of a group of muscles

slides (slydez) *noun* small glass plates on which specimens are examined

specimens (SPES-uh-menz) *noun* small samples

sterile (STAIR-uhl) *adjective* unable to have children

symptoms (SIMP-tuhmz) *noun* health conditions that indicate disease

syringe (sih-RINJ) *noun* a medical instrument used for injecting fluids

T

toxic (TOK-sik) *adjective* describing something harmful or destructive, such as poison

transmitted (trans-MIT-id) *verb* passed onto someone or something else

tumor (TOO-mur) *noun* a growth of tissue, sometimes caused by disease

X

x-ray (EX-ray) *noun* a picture that a doctor takes of the inside of a patient's body

Index

Author's Note

Sometimes, being a writer is like being a detective. You need to do a lot of research, uncover facts, and find the people and evidence (material) you need to "solve your case."

For instance, when I was assigned to write this book about parasites, I needed to gather evidence so, one of the first things I did was read books by experts on the subject. One of the most intriguing was written by an infectious disease specialist named Dr. Pamela Nagami. It's called *The Woman with a Worm in Her Head*. I knew I had to track down the author for an interview.

It just so happened I met a colleague of hers at my son's basketball game. He told me he'd get me her e-mail address the next day.

I e-mailed Dr. Nagami three days before Christmas. Even with her incredibly hectic schedule, she agreed to an interview.

My next bit of sleuthing came about because of an article about guinea worms in the *New York Times* on Sunday, March 26, 2006. It was a story by writer Donald McNeil Jr. explaining how villagers in a remote part of Nigeria were getting infected with guinea worms.

The Scholastic editors read the story, too, and decided to include a guinea worm case in this book. Now I needed to find the sources, beginning with Mr. McNeil. First I went on the *New York Times* Web site and found an e-mail address for news editors.

Within 24 hours I received this response from McNeil: "I understand you are trying to reach me. I am writing two articles for tonight's paper on malaria and avian flu, so I can't talk right now. But if you want to reach me tomorrow, we can talk then." The next day, I called McNeil, and he referred me to his main contact at the Carter Center in Atlanta, Georgia. It was Emily Staub, the assistant director in the Office of Public Information for Health Programs.

Emily was eager to help and arranged a phone meeting with Aryc (pronounced Eric) Mosher, the assistant director of the guinea worm program at the Carter Center. It was Aryc who provided the history for this book's guinea worm case in Ghana.

Reporting is an exciting job. You get to learn new things and meet and talk to fascinating people. You can play detective, too!

ACKNOWLEDGMENTS

I would like to thank the following people. Without their help, this book would not be possible: Dr. Pamela Nagami, Aryc Mosher, Dr. Tiffany Grunwald, Dr. Rehka Murthy, Dr. Michael Flagg, Emily Staub, Thomas D. Lewis, Shelly Fredman, Dr. Lisa Chan Flagg

CONTENT ADVISER: Mark S. Dworkin, MD, MPH & TM, Associate Professor, Division of Epidemiology and Biostatistics, University of Illinois at Chicago